# Learning to Slow Down and Pay Attention

Published by
MAGINATION PRESS
An Educational Publishing Foundation Book
American Psychological Association
750 First Street, NE
Washington, DC 20002

For more information about our books, including a complete catalog, please write to us,
call 1-800-374-2721, or visit our website at www.maginationpress.com.

Printed by Worzalla, Stevens Point, Wisconsin
Cover design by Tiffany McCord
Book design by Susan K. White

Library of Congress Cataloging-in-Publication Data

Nadeau, Kathleen G.
Learning to slow down and pay attention : a book for kids about ADHD / written by
Kathleen G. Nadeau and Ellen B. Dixon ; illustrated by Charles Beyl.—3rd ed.
p. cm.
Includes bibliographical references.
ISBN 1-59147-149-4 (hardcover : alk. paper) — ISBN 1-59147-155-9 (pbk. : alk. paper)
1. Attention-deficit hyperactivity disorder—Juvenile literature. 2. Attention-deficit-
disordered children—Juvenile literature. [1. Attention-deficit hyperactivity disorder.]
I. Dixon, Ellen B. II. Beyl, Charles, ill. III. Title.
RJ506.H9N33 2004
618.92'8589—dc22                                                             2003028200

Manufactured in the United States of America
10 9 8

# Learning to Slow Down and Pay Attention

## A BOOK FOR KIDS ABOUT ADHD

THIRD EDITION

written by Kathleen G. Nadeau, Ph.D.
and Ellen B. Dixon, Ph.D.

illustrated by Charles Beyl

MAGINATION PRESS • WASHINGTON, DC

# Contents

PART THREE

# THINGS I CAN DO TO HELP MYSELF

PART FOUR

# SPECIAL PROJECTS WITH MY PARENTS

# To Parents
# and Other Adult Helpers

**Many** parents ask, "What do I tell my child about ADHD?" They want to help their child understand ADHD in a realistic, positive, and constructive way. This book is designed as the perfect learning tool to help parents guide their child as he or she confronts the challenges of ADHD. *Learning to Slow Down and Pay Attention* is unique because it is kid-centered, written from the child's point of view. As one boy told us, "This book understands me."

*Learning to Slow Down* is ADHD-friendly: illustrated with cartoons to hold your child's interest, highly readable (even for kids who don't like to read), and divided into sections, so that the book can be read in smaller portions. It is intended for elementary school aged children.

We've divided this book into four parts: A Checklist About Me, Things Other People Can Do to Help Me, Things I Can Do to Help Myself, and Special Projects with My Parents. We suggest that you read the book along with your child and that you go through only one section at a sitting, pausing to discuss various points and ideas whenever this seems useful.

The third part, which focuses on things that children can learn to do to help themselves, should be used repeatedly as a reference while your child gradually builds ADHD coping skills.

A fun activity page is included at the end of each section. In this way, your child can complete each section on a relaxed and upbeat note.

There is a great deal of variety among children who are currently labeled ADHD. Some are hyperactive and impulsive, while others are more quiet and distractible. Other children have significant attentional difficulties but don't meet the strict criteria for an ADHD diagnosis. All of these children are in great need of assistance and intervention, and this book is designed to help.

In this new, third edition of *Learning to Slow Down and Pay Attention*, we have made a number of changes to reflect changes in our understanding of ADHD and in our approach to its treatment. For example, in response to growing research on the safety and efficacy of stimulant medication in treating ADHD, we explain more to the child about medication and how it works. Another important change in this edition is that we've increased our child-centered focus. While the majority of what's written about ADHD emphasizes behaviors that bother adults, we've increased our emphasis on those aspects of ADHD that are troublesome to the children, trying to look at the world more from *their* point of view.

We hope this new edition will be an enjoyable way for your child to learn about him- or herself and to begin the life-long process of self-understanding and self-help.

— **Kathleen Nadeau, Ph.D., and Ellen Dixon, Ph.D.**

# Just for Kids!

**Some** kids have trouble paying attention in school or finishing their homework at night. Some of these kids are very active and have trouble sitting still. Others have their minds on a million things that are more interesting than school, so they can't keep their minds on their schoolwork. They may forget things or lose things, or get in trouble because they do something without stopping to think.

Having problems like these can be tough. It's hard to spend all day in school, and even harder to get homework done at night. Sometimes kids have trouble getting along with other kids, or feel as if somebody is always mad at them.

If you have any of these difficulties, this book can help. There are lots of things that can make these problems better. Some things you can do for yourself. You can also get help from your parents, your teachers, your doctor, your counselor, or a special tutor. We'd like you to read this book with your parents or some other adult so that you can talk to them about what you read.

The kids we've described have something we call Attention-Deficit/Hyperactivity Disorder, or ADHD. You might have heard of ADHD before. (Sometimes it's just called ADD.) Kids who have ADHD have what some people call a "sleepy brain." That means that some parts of your brain–the parts that help you think before you act, that help you sit still and pay attention (even when it's boring), the parts that help you remember and be organized– are a little "sleepy" and don't always work as well as you want them to.

Sometimes the reason that school is so hard for these kids is that it seems boring. Kids with ADHD like to do interesting and exciting things, and school isn't always exciting or interesting.

What you probably haven't heard about is that lots of kids with ADHD are smart and creative. You also probably haven't heard that there are some very famous and successful people who have this thing called ADHD.

Your parents bought this book because they want to help you feel good about yourself and have a better time in school, with your friends, and at home.

We'd love to hear from you after you read this book. Let us know what you think. There are lots of books about ADHD for parents and teachers, but we thought that kids deserve to have their own book. So this one is just for you!

Lots of kids (and some grownups, too) have trouble paying attention because it's hard for them to sit still and listen.

- Do you ever feel as if your motor is running, even when you're sitting still?

- Do you feel like wiggling and fidgeting when you have to sit and listen to your teacher?

- Do you talk a lot and have trouble being quiet in class?

- Do you forget to raise your hand and wait for the teacher to call on you?

- Is it hard to wait your turn?

- Do you play around and bump into other kids when you're waiting in line?

If you answer yes to lots of these questions, you have a lot of energy! And having so much energy can make it hard to settle down and pay attention in school.

Some kids draw and doodle in class because it's too hard to do nothing while they listen. Some kids sit at their desk and try to pay attention, but pretty soon their imagination takes over and they're not listening to what's happening in class, like this...

If you have trouble paying attention in school, do you think you're like the kids who are fidgety and talkative, or like the kids who are quiet and lost in their thoughts? You could be a little like both. Ask your mom or dad what they think. Kids with ADHD usually have trouble paying attention, being organized, remembering what they're supposed to do, and keeping track of things.

No two kids with ADHD are exactly alike. The next section of our book tells you some of the things that kids with ADHD have said about themselves. We would like you to read each comment with your mom or dad. Make a check mark in the box next to each one that you think is just like you. Like this:

After you have finished checking off the things that describe you, we'll tell you ways that you can help yourself be successful in school, and get along better with your friends and family. And we'll also tell you how your parents and the other adults in your life can help.

# A Checklist About Me

**The** following checklist is a collection of things that other kids with ADHD have said about themselves. Going through this checklist can help you think more clearly about yourself—at school, with your friends, and at home. It will help you understand the things that you are very good at and the things that you're having problems with. Going over your answers with your mom or dad is a good way to start talking with your parents about all of these things. And these checklists will help you understand yourself and ADHD better.

# AT SCHOOL

- [ ] When I'm at school,
  it's hard to sit still at my desk.

- [ ] I forget to raise my hand.

- [ ] I can't seem to keep my books
  and papers organized.

- [ ] I often forget my assignments.

- [ ] I have trouble getting started on my work
  in class.

- [ ] Teachers are always telling me,
  "Slow down, don't rush!"

- [ ] My desk is usually a big mess.
- [ ] I forget to hand in my homework.
- [ ] I have trouble remembering the directions the teacher gives us.
- [ ] Even when I try to listen, sometimes I start thinking about something else.
- [ ] A lot of the time I feel bored in class.
- [ ] I'd like school a lot more if I could work on things I'm interested in.
- [ ] I'm afraid that my teacher will be mad at me if I don't finish my work on time.
- [ ] I feel embarrassed when the teacher calls on me and I haven't been listening.

- [ ] I make mistakes in my schoolwork, even though I know the right way to do it.

- [ ] My handwriting is pretty messy.

- [ ] I think I'm pretty smart when I get to do the things I like.

- [ ] I think I've got a good imagination.

- [ ] I'd like school a lot more if you could get up and DO things instead of just sitting at your desk.

- [ ] School can be fun when we get to talk about our ideas and do interesting projects.

- [ ] My teacher says I bother the other kids too much.

- [ ] I never seem to finish my seat work as quickly as the other kids.

- [ ] Sometimes I get in trouble for talking in class.

## WITH OTHER KIDS

☐ Sometimes I get angry at other kids, and I start name-calling or even fighting.

☐ My feelings are hurt very easily—more than other kids'.

☐ Sometimes other kids complain to the teacher that I'm bothering them.

☐ Some of my friends are younger than I am.

☐ I don't know why, but sometimes other kids don't want to play with me.

- [ ] Some kids think I'm really funny, but the teacher gets mad at me for joking around.

- [ ] My mom or dad tells me I'm too bossy with other kids.

- [ ] Sometimes kids pick on me and tease me.

- [ ] I wish I had more friends.

- [ ] Sometimes I feel sad and left out.

- [ ] Sometimes other kids tease me and call me names.

- [ ] It's easy to be friends at first, but pretty soon they're not my friends anymore.

## ABOUT MYSELF

- [ ] My life would be wonderful if there was no such thing as school.

- [ ] I worry that I'm not as smart as other kids in reading or writing or math.

- [ ] Sometimes I think I'm smart and school is dumb!

- [ ] I want other kids to like me more.

- [ ] Sometimes I think something is wrong with me, but I don't know what it is.

- [ ] I wish I didn't get upset so easily.

- [ ] I feel frustrated because my schoolwork takes so long.

- [ ] It would be great if I could remember what I've learned when I'm taking a test.
- [ ] I lose things and forget things, no matter how hard I try not to.
- [ ] It feels like people get mad at me no matter what I do.
- [ ] I hate it when people tease me.
- [ ] Sometimes I feel different from the other kids –kind of left out.
- [ ] I wish my parents and my teachers would notice more of the GOOD things about me!

## AT HOME

☐ Sometimes I don't hear my parents call me and they think I'm just ignoring them.

☐ I have lots of arguments with my brother or sister.

☐ It feels like my parents pick on me more than anyone else in my family.

☐ I always have trouble getting started on homework.

☐ I have lots of trouble getting up and ready for school on time.

☐ I forget to do things I've been told, and my parents think I'm doing it on purpose.

☐ I hate to be bugged about doing homework and chores.

☐ There never seems to be much time to do stuff that I like to do.

☐ My room is a big mess.

☐ I have trouble falling asleep at night.

☐ I worry about school and sometimes get stomachaches and wish I could stay home.

☐ It seems like I'm always in trouble for something.

## WHAT I WISH OTHER PEOPLE KNEW

- ☐ I really do care about my schoolwork.
- ☐ I don't lose or forget things on purpose.
- ☐ I hate it when people tell me I'm not trying.
- ☐ Lots of the time it's really confusing to be me.
- ☐ I don't mean to do things that get other kids mad at me.
- ☐ I want my mom and dad to be proud of me.

**Congratulations!** You've finished the checklist. Have you talked to your mom or dad about your answers? Were they surprised by any of your answers? Did your mom or dad tell you that they had some of the same feelings when they were a kid? It may feel like you've checked off a lot of problems in this section, but…

## DON'T WORRY!

## HELP IS ON THE WAY!

The rest of this book will tell you about ways that you can feel better when you're in school, with other kids, and at home with your family. There are lots of ways that other people can help you, and ways that you can learn to help yourself.

Now, if you're like a lot of the kids who helped us write this book, you're getting a little tired of reading right now. That's OK. It's good to take a break after you concentrate for a while. ("Concentrate" means trying really hard to pay attention.)

## Time for a break!

Why don't you take a break now and see if you can help our heroes find their homework? We bet you know how they feel!

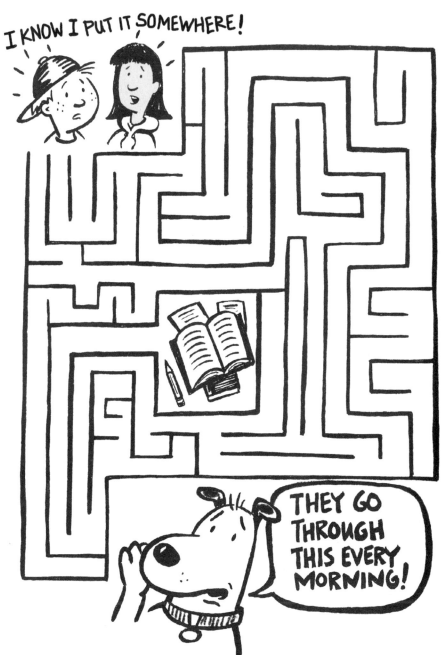

Do you feel better after your break? Taking a short break when you're tired is a good habit to learn. Whenever you're doing schoolwork, you will get more done if you concentrate hard and then give yourself a five-minute break every 15 or 20 minutes. You can have your mom or dad set a timer so that you know when your five-minute break is over.

# Things Other People Can Do to Help Me

**Lots** of kids have trouble in school—getting distracted, not finishing class work, having trouble with reading and remembering what they've read.  Some of them also have trouble getting along with other kids. Often they feel frustrated at home, too—arguing with their parents, or feeling sad and discouraged.

If you have any of these kinds of problems, there are lots of adults who can help. There are counselors who can help you learn how to get along better with your friends and family. There are tutors and coaches who can help you learn to get your schoolwork done more quickly, and help you learn better. There are also special doctors who can help kids pay better attention.

# People Who Help with School

**Someone** who really understands your problems, such as a counselor or a tutor, might go to your school and talk to your teacher about ways to help you to become a better student. For some kids, it helps to work in a quieter place, or to go to a school with smaller classes. When there are fewer distractions, kids can concentrate better.

# People Who Help with Friends and Feelings

**Sometimes** it is helpful for kids to see a counselor who can teach them how to make friends and how to get along better with other kids. You can tell your counselor about problems you have at home or at school and how you feel about them. The counselor never fusses at you and never says it's all your fault.

Counseling can help you understand yourself better and feel more confident, too. If you go to counseling, it would be a good idea to take this book with you. You could show your counselor the things you checked off in the first section of this book, and your counselor could help you figure out what to do.

# People Who Help My Parents Understand Me

**Your** parents might talk with a coach who specializes in helping kids with ADHD or a counselor, too. The coach or counselor can teach your parents better ways to help you get ready for school in the morning, easier ways to help you finish your homework, and better ideas for helping you when you feel angry or frustrated.

Your parents will also learn that you haven't been just lazy or bad. They'll learn that you really have been trying, but that it's hard for you to do what everybody wants you to do.

BOY, IT <u>IS</u> HARD! I'M GLAD SOMEBODY FINALLY FIGURED THAT OUT!

# Doctors Who Help with Medicine

**Some** kids go to a doctor who gives them special medicine that helps them calm down, pay better attention, and get their schoolwork done. Taking medicine doesn't mean you are sick. The medicine just gives your body what it needs so you can pay attention and stay on track. Remember when we talked about "sleepy brains" in ADHD kids? The medicine that doctors usually give to kids with ADHD is called "stimulant medicine." Stimulant

medicine helps kids with ADHD because it helps to wake up—"stimulate"—the parts of their brain that are sleepy. Then they can listen better, remember better, and get their schoolwork done more quickly. ADHD medicine can help you pay better attention to everything, like keeping your eye on the ball in sports, or like listening better to your friends without interrupting.

Some medicine lasts all day, and kids only take it at home in the morning. Other medicine lasts a few hours, so kids might need to go to the nurse at school to take more during the school day.

As you can see, there are lots of different ways that other people can help you. But you can also do lots of things to help yourself. On the following pages are some ideas that you can try at home or at school. You'll need to talk about them with your parents and teachers so that they can help you.

**But now you're probably ready for another break!**

# CONNECT THE DOTS AND YOU WILL SEE WHY HE'S AS PLEASED AS HE CAN BE!

# Things I Can Do to Help Myself

**There** are lots of ways to get help—your parents and teachers can help, and medicine can help—but some of the most important ways are things that you can learn to do yourself. It's important to get help from others as you're learning these new habits. They'll take time and lots of practice before you do them automatically. Your mom or dad or a counselor can help you decide what to work on first and can help you remember to keep practicing.

# Ways to Remember

**Most** kids who have trouble paying attention also have trouble remembering things. If this is true for you, here are some tips:

- Write yourself a note. Colored stick pads are great because you can stick notes where you will be sure to see them.

- It can be hard to remember things you're told. Ask your mom or dad to write you a note and stick the note where you'll see it.

- Always put things in the same place: a hook for your jacket, a shelf for books and backpack, a box for shoes and soccer balls. If these are all together in a convenient place, you can easily put your things away when you come in the house. That way you'll know where they are when you need them!

- Set the kitchen timer as a reminder. For example, if you need to leave for swimming practice in 20 minutes, set the timer to remind you when to go.

- Learn to do it now! When you think of something, do it right away. Then you won't have time to forget.

- If you need to take something to school, put it in one special place by the door.

- Learn to stop and think for a minute before you rush out the door. "Let's see, have I got everything I need?"

Keep track of your activities and the things you need to do with a calendar and a "Things to Do" list next to it on a bulletin board.

Hang your bulletin board where you'll see it often. In many families, the kitchen is a good place to hang your calendar and your "Things to Do" list.

Each day, check your calendar and your list of things to remember. Your mom or dad can help.

Think about your day when you wake up. "Let's see, today is Tuesday, so I have soccer practice after school. I need to take my soccer cleats."

# Getting Ready in the Morning

**The** best way to get ready in the morning is to prepare as much as you can the night before. That way, if something is lost, you'll have time to look for it.

- Put out your clothes the night before.

- Pack your lunch the night before.

- Get together everything you'll need to take to school the next day, such as lunch money, homework, and permission slips.

- In the morning, have a regular routine. Doing things in the same order each morning makes it easier to get it done.

- Make a checklist of what to do each morning and put it on the wall where you will see it. Check it several times while you're getting ready.

- Don't play or watch TV until you're completely ready!

- Get your mom or dad to set up a "launching pad." This is a place for you to put everything you'll take to school the next day. Make a list near your launching pad of what you'll need.

# The Easy Way to Clean a Bedroom

**If** you're like lots of kids, your mom or dad is always bugging you, "Clean up your room!" Cleaning your room probably isn't your idea of fun. Probably you only clean your room when your parents insist. But did you know that a clean room can help you feel better and do better in school?

When your room is clean, you can find what you need. This will help you get to school on time and even remember to take your homework to school to turn in. When your room is neat, you can focus better on reading or homework and get it done more quickly!

# 8 STEPS TO A CLEAN ROOM!

**You will need:**

 Trash can

Four cardboard boxes labeled
TOY BOX, BOOK BOX, SCHOOL BOX,
and SHOE BOX

 Clothes hamper

Two hooks in your closet

 Some shelves

Desk

## HERE'S WHAT YOU DO:

 **STEP 1** Put all the dirty clothes in the hamper and all the clean clothes in your dresser.

 **STEP 2** Put all the toys on the shelves and in the box labeled "toy box."

 **STEP 3** Put all the books on a shelf or in the "book box."

 **STEP 4** Put all the school stuff and backpack on your desk or in your "school box."

 **STEP 5** Put all the shoes in your closet or in the "shoe box."

**STEP 6** Put all the trash and throw-away stuff in the trash can or a garbage bag.

 **STEP 7** Make your bed.

 **STEP 8** Hang your pajamas and your coat on hooks in the closet.

If you do this one step at a time, you'll soon be an expert at cleaning up your own bedroom! Your mom or dad could even make a checklist with these eight steps and get it copied, so that you could use one each week.

# Ways to Pay Better Attention at School

**Paying** attention is important if you want to learn and do well in school. And the better you do in school, the better you'll feel about yourself. Here are a few tips that can help you pay better attention in school.

- Sit close to the front of the class, and look at your teacher whenever he or she is talking.

- Get involved! Don't just sit there. Ask questions and make comments (after raising your hand, of course).

- Keep your desk clear, so you're working on only one thing at a time.

- Ask to be moved away from kids who talk or bother you, and don't talk when you should be listening.

- To remind yourself to pay attention, wear a rubber band on your wrist and give it a little snap if you start daydreaming. But don't shoot it!

- If your class is too noisy or distracting while you're trying to work, ask the teacher if you can move your desk or sit in a quiet place.

- Don't bring to school toys or games that will distract you.

- If you don't understand something, ask for help right away.

# Things to Do If I Feel Fidgety

**It's** hard to pay attention and get your schoolwork done when you feel fidgety. Here are some tips to help you feel better when you have the fidgets.

- Ask the teacher if you can run an errand or help with something for a few minutes. Then go back to your work.

- Ask if you can keep a koosh ball in your desk to squeeze at times when you're not doing schoolwork. (But never toss it or throw it!)

- Ask your mom or dad in advance if you may leave the dinner table as soon as you have finished eating.

- Get some exercise every day—playing outside, taking a walk with your mom or dad, or going to karate lessons or to sports practice.

- Stand up and s-t-r-e-t-ch. Then bend over and touch your toes. Then sit back down. Do this quietly.

- Take a five-minute break if you're doing homework, or spend a few minutes memorizing things while walking around the table.

- Draw pictures at your desk, if you have finished your work.

# Help with Homework

**Some** kids take a long time to finish their homework. Here are some helpful hints to get it done right and to get it done sooner.

## DEVELOP A HOMEWORK HABIT

Think about the time of day when you can get your homework done best. Usually, it's a time when you're not too tired. Think about the place in your house where you can work best. Maybe it's at the kitchen table where you can ask your mom or dad a question while they're cooking dinner. Or maybe you work best at the dining room table after dinner, away from the TV where it's quiet. Talk to your mom or dad about what they think. If you're not sure, try doing homework at different times (after school or after dinner) and in different places (your bedroom, the kitchen table, the dining room).

Think about whether you get your work done best when you're alone or when you have a parent nearby to help. Some kids work best when there is a specific "homework time"–when brothers and sisters are doing homework too. Think about whether you get your homework done better if you take a second dose of medicine in the afternoon so that it is still working while you do your homework.

When you decide on the best time and place, then work on developing a homework habit. A habit is something you do the same way each time. After a week or two of sitting down at the same time in the same place, you'll find that it's much easier to get your homework done because you've trained your brain to get down to work and stay focused.

## MORE HOMEWORK HELP

Here are some more tips to help you get your homework done...and handed in!

- Keep a special assignment notebook so that you can write your assignments down when your teacher gives them.

- If you're not sure you have all your assignments, ask your teacher to check your homework list at the end of the day.

- Find a quiet place to do homework that's away from temptations like TV.

- Do your homework when you're not too tired. Some kids do better if they play after school and do their homework after dinner. Other kids are too tired to do homework after dinner. Think about the best time for you.

- If you get tired of sitting, try standing up for a minute while you read.

- Some kids learn better if they talk out loud and walk around the room while they memorize things like math facts.

- Reward yourself for finishing your homework. A snack or favorite activity is a great reward to look forward to.

- Don't try to do too much at one time. Work for 15 minutes, take a short break, then work some more.

- Have a special, brightly colored homework folder that you keep in your backpack. As soon as you've finished a homework assignment, put it in this folder. That way, it will be easy to find and turn in the next day.

# Learning to Control My Anger

**Getting** frustrated and angry is a problem for lots of kids. Everyone gets angry sometimes–that's natural. But getting angry can cause problems if it happens too much or if you don't know how to handle it very well. You can lose friends, get in trouble at school, or have a hard time getting along with your family. Do you become angry more than most other kids?

Here are some things you can do to keep from getting too angry or upset.

- Go away from the person you're mad at so you can think first, before you say or do something that will hurt someone or get you in trouble.

- If someone is trying to make you angry, be smart. Don't let them get you in trouble. Go tell your parent or your teacher about the problem.

- Stay away from anyone who picks on you or tries to get you upset.

- If something you're doing, like homework, is frustrating you, ask for help right away, before you get really fed up.

- If you're angry because you are not allowed to do something you want to do, ask if there's a way you can earn it as a reward.

- If you are too angry to talk without yelling, try talking about the problem to someone you are not mad at. Talking calmly about a problem can help you think about it and maybe find a solution.

- Do something to get your angry feelings out— like kicking a ball in the backyard or running around outside for a few minutes.

- Find a quiet place, if you can, to do the Calm Down Exercise described on the next page.

# CALM DOWN EXERCISE

When you're really frustrated and feel like you might lose it, try the Calm Down Exercise. It has three parts.

1. Think of something you like—listening to music, going to the beach, or riding your bike. Try to get a good picture of this in your mind.
2. Take a deep breath and let it out very slowly.
3. Think the words "calm down."

Okay, let's try it. First think of something nice. Now take a deep breath and let it out very s-l-o-w-l-y and think "calm down." Now do it two more times. **YOU DID IT. TERRIFIC!**

Remember, when you're really angry, you may need to do this at least three times. Then, if you're still angry or frustrated, go find a parent or teacher to help you with your problems.

It helps to practice the Calm Down Exercise first, when you're not angry. Maybe your mother or father would practice it with you. It might help them too!

# Learning to Ask for Help

**What** do you do when you're confused or when something is too hard for you? Some kids feel embarrassed when they don't know what to do. Instead of asking for help, they sit there and don't let anyone know. This only makes the problem worse. It's okay if you forget something or don't understand something. Just go to your teacher or your mom or dad and say something like:

**"I forgot what you asked me to do."**

*or*

**"Will you help me with this?"**

*or*

**"Will you explain that again?"**

*or*

**"Will you show me what you mean?"**

Explain that you are trying hard. Tell your teacher that one way you help yourself is by making sure you understand what you need to do.

# Talking Out Problems at Home

**Do** you feel like your mom or dad is on your case all the time? Do problems at home usually turn into arguments? It really helps to make a regular time to talk out problems with your parents. If you have lots of arguments with a brother or sister, this could be a good time to talk about those problems, too.

Don't try to talk about a problem when you're really upset. Wait until you have calmed down. It's good to have a regular time to talk about problems or disagreements in the family. Pick a time when everyone is home and has time to sit down and listen. Try to do this once a week. If there is a big disagreement that can't wait for the weekly meeting, then try to sit down and talk that same day—but be sure to wait until you're feeling calmer!

Talking about problems means explaining how you feel, listening to others, trying to understand how they feel, and then looking for solutions.

**Here are some rules for Family Talk Time:**

- Everyone should have a chance to say how they feel about the problem.

- No interrupting.

- Don't talk for too long. Say what you think in a few sentences and let other people have their turn.

- Don't blame or call names. You are looking for solutions, not new problems!

- Try to come up with some new ideas.

- Listen to the ideas of your parents.

- Try new ideas for a few days, and then talk again to discuss how these ideas are working. Then you can make changes or come up with completely new ideas if the old ones don't solve the problem.

If you and your family have a regular problem-solving time, things will probably be a lot calmer and nicer at your house!

# Problem Solving

**What** do you do when you have a problem? For really big problems, you may need the help of a parent or teacher, but sometimes you can figure out what to do all by yourself by using these steps:

 What's the problem? (For example, I forget to hand in homework.)

 What are some of the things I could do about the problem? (I could ask my friend to remind me. I could get a fluorescent folder to put my homework in. I could stick a note on my desk…)

 Which one seems best? (Stick the reminder note on my desk.)

 Try out your idea and see if it works. (Yeah! I saw my note and handed in my homework!)

 If it doesn't work, try another one of your ideas. (Oops! I forgot to write the note. Maybe I'll ask Dad to buy me a fluorescent folder to keep my homework in. That way I'll notice the folder and turn in my homework.)

Think of a problem you have now, or that you have had in the past few days. Try problem solving using all five steps, and see if you can think of a solution that you haven't found before. Maybe your mom or dad could help you practice problem solving.

Try keeping a family journal of problems and solutions. Your mom or dad can help you with this journal. Then bring the journal to future family discussions. That way, you can remember what solutions worked and what solutions didn't work, and everyone can remember the new idea they're going to try.

# Learning Not to Interrupt

**Some** kids have a big problem with interrupting other people. All people interrupt, but some kids interrupt almost constantly. If you do this, the people you are talking to become very annoyed and may even decide they don't want to be friends with you. Here are a few things you can do.

- If you have to say something, ask permission. "Can I say something for just a second?" or "Excuse me, may I ask a question?"

- Really think about what the other person is saying. Pretend there will be a quiz in five minutes and you will be asked to repeat every word that person has said.

- If you interrupt, apologize.

- Wait until the other person ends his or her sentence before you start talking.

Not interrupting is something you can practice at home. Make it into a game. See how long you can last at dinner without interrupting.

# Ways to Make and Keep Friends

**Everyone** wants to have friends, but some kids are better at making and keeping friends. If you wish you had more friends, or if you have lots of disagreements with your friends, here are some things that can help.

- Look friendly, smile, and say "hi."

- Share your stuff when you're playing with friends.

- Take turns. Let everybody get a chance to play with a toy or be a leader.

- Don't be bossy. Let other kids help make some of the decisions.

- Keep calm. Don't get too silly or too loud.

- Say nice things to your friends, like "Good catch!" or "Nice try!"

- Try not to poke, grab, or bump into your friends.

- Don't ever make fun of anybody. You know how awful that feels.

- Don't hit, yell, or call names if you feel angry. Remember to walk away and calm down so that you won't say or do something you'll feel bad about later.

- If you have a big problem with a friend, call an adult to help solve it. If you have a little problem, try to work it out with your friend!

- Say you're sorry if you've said or done something that hurts someone's feelings.

# Things to Do When Someone Hurts My Feelings

**Some** kids' feelings are easily hurt. This can be a big problem, because there are lots of kids who will pick on you even more if they know they can get you upset. It's never fun to be picked on, but here are a few things that might help:

- Ignore them. It's not much fun for teasers to pick on someone who doesn't react.

- Stand up for yourself. Don't lose your temper, but tell them in a firm voice to "cut it out!"

- If there are children who pick on you over and over, try to stay away from them. If they won't let you stay away from them, tell an adult right away before the problem gets worse. An adult can help you solve the problem.

- Talk to a friend or counselor. When our feelings are hurt, it can really help to talk to someone else about it.

- Look for kids who are friendly and positive. Don't keep trying to make friends with someone who is mean or who criticizes you all the time.

# Learning to Relax

**Kids** sometimes feel very stressed because they are tired or hungry, or they have had a hard day at school. These are times when fights and arguments are most likely to happen. When you feel stressed, practice some of these ways to relax. These are good ideas for grownups, too!

- Go to your room and lie down, or do something quiet.

- Eat a small snack if you are hungry.

- Stay away from your brother or sister if you are fighting with him or her.

- Take a warm bath.

- Listen to quiet, calm music.

- Take a walk with your mom or dad.

- Curl up with your dog or cat.

- Ask your mom or dad for a backrub if you're really stressed out about something.

- Do one of your favorite activities.

- Do something creative—like drawing, painting, or building something—to get your mind off your worries.

- Do something physical—like riding your bike or going outside and bouncing a basketball.

# When I Have Trouble Going to Sleep

**Some** kids have a lot of trouble relaxing at night so that they can fall asleep. This can be a big problem because if you have trouble sleeping at night, you will be tired the next day. And when you are tired, your difficulties with paying attention, remembering, and doing your schoolwork will be worse. Not getting enough sleep makes it harder to get along with your friends and family, because when you're tired you're more likely to feel grumpy or get angry and frustrated more easily.

Here are some things that can help you fall asleep more easily.

- Have a very regular evening schedule, and do things in the same order. For example:

6:30 p.m. Do homework in a room away from the TV.

7:30 p.m. Have a snack and watch a half-hour of TV.

8:00 p.m. Get ready for tomorrow—make lunch, pick out clothes.

8:15 p.m. Take a bath, brush teeth, and put on pajamas.

8:30 p.m. Get in bed and read a book or have story time with Mom or Dad.

9:00 p.m. Goodnight kiss and lights out.

- Avoid doing anything really active or exciting on school nights.

- Play soft music after your light is turned off.

- Don't watch TV or listen to your favorite rock station. That will just keep you awake longer.

- Try reading a homework assignment. That can sometimes make you go to sleep in five minutes!

- Don't take naps during the day or sleep late in the morning. That makes it hard to get to sleep on time at night.

- If you are taking stimulant medicine to help you pay better attention, make sure you don't take it too late in the day.

● Don't drink anything with caffeine in the afternoon or evening. If you're not sure what has caffeine, ask your mom or dad.

● If you don't fall asleep right away, just relax, keep your eyes closed, and try having some "awake dreams," sort of like watching a movie in your head. Imagine that you are in one of your favorite places (like maybe at the beach) and then imagine what you'd be doing (like building a sand castle or taking a walk along the edge of the water).

# Things I Want to Change

**Boy**, that's a lot of stuff to try and learn how to do! We've talked about lots of different things you can do to make your life happier and go more smoothly. Don't try to learn how to do all of these things at once. You and your parents should decide on one thing to change. Practice it for a while. When that change is easy for you, then start working on a new one.

On the next page, make a list of the things you want to change first.

# THINGS I WANT TO CHANGE!

_____

_____

_____

_____

_____

_____

_____

_____

_____

_____

Later, Part Four of our book talks about ways that you and your parents can work together on making these changes. If you work together it can be a lot of fun, and you will feel very good about yourself when you succeed!

# Ways to Feel Good About Me

**Some** kids start to feel bad about themselves because their teachers and parents criticize them and because they may have problems with other kids. After a while you may feel so discouraged that you think there is nothing good about you. Here are some things you can do to feel good about yourself.

- Make a list of things you like about yourself. Ask your mom and dad to add things to your list, too. You can start your list on the next page!

- Look for people who are nice and who encourage you.

- Look for things to do that you can be good at doing.

- If your mom or dad criticizes you a lot, this is a good thing to talk about in a family problem-solving session.

- Have a "special time" every day with your mom or dad—a time when you just hang out or do something fun, a time when you don't talk about problems.

- Talk to a counselor about your feelings.

- When you feel discouraged, encourage yourself by saying things like:

> **"Nobody is good at everything.**
> **I may have trouble with _____,**
> **but I'm really good at _____."**
>
> *or*
>
> **"I may feel bad right now,**
> **but there are lots of things I can do**
> **to feel better—like talking to someone**
> **who really understands and likes me."**
>
> *or*
>
> **"This is a problem,**
> **but I'm a good problem solver."**
>
> *or*
>
> **"Everyone makes mistakes.**
> **It's what you do about them that counts."**

# AWESOME THINGS ABOUT ME!

Here's a good place to start your list of things that you like about yourself!

_____

_____

_____

_____

_____

_____

_____

_____

_____

_____

_____

_____

WE'RE GONNA NEED MORE THAN 1 PAGE!

# Finally! It's time for a break!

Remember, it's not good to try to work all the time. We've talked about a lot of things you can work on, but now it's time for a little fun.

See if you can find all the X's in the picture. Circle the letter above each X, and put them all together to find a secret message.

_ _ _ _ _ _ _ _ _ _ _ _ _ _ _ _ _

# Special Projects with My Parents

**It's** really important to get help from your mom or dad when you try to change a habit or behavior. Changing behaviors isn't easy, especially at first, so it helps if your mom or dad works with you. They can encourage you and help you remember the new habit that you're working on. Sometimes they can help you figure out how you're going to develop your new habit, too.

# Working on Changes Together

**Let's** say you decide to change your "getting ready in the morning" habit. Your mom or dad can help you decide on a good morning routine and help you make a checklist. It can also be part of their routine the night before to ask you about permission slips and other information from school that they need to know about.

Whatever habit you pick, your mom or dad can help you think of ways to remind yourself about it. Sometimes it can be fun if your mom or dad tries to work on a new habit at the same time. Then you can remind and encourage each other!

**Here are some tips on working on changes together:**

- Look at your "Things I Want to Change" list on page 76. You might want to pick one of those things to work on, or you may decide to work on something else.

- Pick one project. You may want to work on several, but start with just one. You can get to the others one at a time. This is important so you don't try to do too much and then give up.

- Don't pick something hard at first. Pick something sort of easy and get some practice at learning new behaviors.

- Reward yourself each time you succeed.

- Decide with your parents on the rewards you will earn. Pick a small reward that you can earn each time you are successful. Pick a larger reward that you can earn at the end of the week if you have been successful for a certain number of days that week.

- Don't expect to be perfect. Just try to improve. Remember that little setbacks are normal, and don't feel discouraged when you don't win a reward. New habits take time to build!

- Keep a picture in your mind of how your life will be better when you get that new habit.

- Tell yourself every day, "I can do it!"

# A Progress Chart

**Keep** a daily chart of your progress once you have picked a habit to work on. Decide how well you did that day: getting better? super job? getting off track? You can even have a place on your chart to problem solve if you feel you are getting off track. On page 87 there's an example of a chart that you can use, or you can make a chart of your own.

Talk to your mom or dad every day about your progress. It feels really good to talk about your accomplishments, and it feels good when they are proud of you!

Don't expect to always do a "super job." Nobody is perfect, and nobody changes all at once. Your parents can listen and encourage you, and they can help you problem solve and practice the things you are working hard to learn. If you are having trouble with a special project, talk about the problems with them and try to figure out why. Maybe you picked a project that is too hard at first. Or maybe you and your parents need better reminders to work on your special project every day.

## GOOD LUCK WITH YOUR SPECIAL PROJECTS!

## YOU CAN DO IT!

Week number———

# I'M WORKING ON ————————————

————————————————————————————

## HOW AM I DOING?

|  | Off Track | Getting Better | Super Job! |
|---|---|---|---|
| Day 1 | ☐ | ☐ | ☐ |
| Day 2 | ☐ | ☐ | ☐ |
| Day 3 | ☐ | ☐ | ☐ |
| Day 4 | ☐ | ☐ | ☐ |
| Day 5 | ☐ | ☐ | ☐ |
| Day 6 | ☐ | ☐ | ☐ |
| Day 7 | ☐ | ☐ | ☐ |

## PROBLEM SOLVING

When I'm trying to————————————————

———————————————— but I get off track...

What's the problem?————————————————

————————————————————————————

What are some things I can do to try to solve the problem?

1.————————————————————————

2.————————————————————————

3.————————————————————————

## You finished the book!

We've covered many things in this book. We hope that you've learned a lot and that you've had some fun, too.

Here's a little reward for all your hard work. Remember, it's always a good idea to reward yourself for a job well done!

# Notes to Parents

**The** more that you know about effective behavior management of children with ADHD, the more useful this book will be for you and your child. Here we have listed ways to reward your child, ways to build a positive relationship, organizations that can help, and a suggested reading list.

## REWARDING YOUR CHILD

Changing habits is hard work. Kids need incentives (not bribes), just as adults do. Rewards don't have to be expensive. Nor should they be anything you don't want to give your child. They need to be things you both feel good about. Often the best rewards—those that kids enjoy the most—are special activities rather than things. Here are some rewards that other parents have used:

- Playing a board game with a parent
- Baking cookies
- Inviting a friend over after school
- Inviting a friend to spend the night on the weekend
- Dinner at the child's favorite restaurant
- Ordering a home-delivery pizza
- Playing a computer game with a parent
- Playing ball for 20 minutes with a parent
- Eliminating a particular chore one evening
- Allowing your child to stay up an extra 15 or 30 minutes one night
- Getting a simple science experiment book and letting your child select one to do with a parent
- Renting a video or DVD and making popcorn
- Making a special snack with a parent
- Going online for half an hour after homework is done

- Allowing your child to pick a small favor from a "grab bag" filled with such things as gum, collector cards, or vending machine toys
- Giving your child a special bedtime backrub
- Reading an extra story at bedtime

When you and your child decide on a special project, it is important to establish the rules before you begin and make sure they are thorough and clear. If your child is expecting one thing, but it turns out you have something else in mind and his expectations aren't met, he can easily grow discouraged.

- Be specific about what is required to earn each reward—for example, how many check marks on a chart.
- Be specific about how the check marks are earned.
- Write all of these rules on the chart and in advance so that they are clear.
- Make it fun. Emphasize improvements, not failures.

Always be generous with encouragement and affection. These are rewards too, and big self-esteem builders—even when the child doesn't appear to notice!

- Smiles
- Hugs
- Pats on the back
- "I like that!"
- "Well done!"
- "Thanks!"
- "Good try!"
- "You're terrific!"

# SPECIAL TIME

It is vitally important that you and your child have good times together. Everyone feels discouraged if they talk only about problems. Plan a "special time" just for fun each day with your child. It can be a few minutes to be together doing something you both enjoy.

Decide together what you want to do. You could play a game, read a book, take a walk, or just talk. It should be fun for both of you—a time to relax, not to change behaviors or to learn new things. Don't use the special time as a "reward" that can be gained or lost. When your child is having behavior problems and has been punished or criticized frequently, it is especially important to have special time together to rebuild positive feelings between you and your child.

## FINDING THE RESOURCES
## YOUR CHILD NEEDS

Many different
types of
professionals can
be helpful to a
child with ADHD.
Specialized tutors,
counselors,
therapists,
ADHD coaches,
knowledgeable
pediatricians, and
child psychiatrists can
all offer professional
expertise that children need to
do their best. Families who are
living in smaller towns may have fewer choices
than those in larger metropolitan areas. However,
professional training and awareness of how to help children
with ADHD is constantly improving.

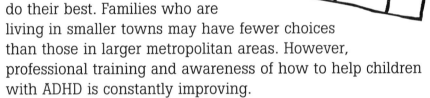

The best way to find resources for your child is to
network with other parents whose children have the same
needs. Internet searches for ADHD resources are sometimes
a good way to get started as well. It may take lots of phone
calls and questions before you find the right professionals
and supports for your child, but it's worth it.

Educate yourself as much as possible. There is a growing
wealth of information available on the internet about ADHD,
as well as in your public library. Join local parent support
groups if they exist. If there are no local support groups,
consider joining forces with other parents to form a group.
Talk to your child's school counselor and/or pediatrician
about community resources.

# HELPFUL WEBSITES

**ADDvance**
**www.ADDvance.com**
This ADHD information and resource site, created by
Kathleen Nadeau, Ph.D., and Patricia Quinn, M.D., contains
special sections for parents, teens, college students, adults,
girls and women, and professionals.

**CHADD (Children and Adults with Attention-Deficit/
Hyperactivity Disorder)**
**www.chadd.org**
This is the nation's largest advocacy organization for people
with ADHD, with more than 20,000 members. CHADD
sponsors local support groups, which can be located on the
CHADD website. CHADD also has a large ADHD resource
center with information on the diagnosis and treatment of
ADHD. Membership includes a subscription to *Attention!*
magazine, published monthly.

**LDA (Learning Disabilities Association of America)**
**www.ldanatl.org**
LDA is the largest non-profit advocacy organization for
individuals with learning disabilities, with over 40,000
members. LDA also sponsors local support groups.
Membership includes a subscription to the LDA newsletter.
LDA has an online bookstore with a wide selection of books
on ADHD, learning disabilities, and related topics.

**LD Online**
**www.ldonline.org**
This website is a well-designed, creative, up-to-date
resource for parents and children about learning disabilities,
ADHD, and related issues, featuring online articles, book
reviews, and resource lists. The site also has a children's
section, "ldonline kidzone," with information, articles,
contests, and many child-friendly materials.

# SUGGESTED READING FOR PARENTS

**ADD/ADHD Behavior-Change Resource Kit,** by Grad Flick, Ph.D. New York: Jossey-Bass, 1998.

**All About Attention Deficit Disorder: Symptoms, Diagnosis and Treatment (2nd ed.),** by Thomas W. Phelan, Ph.D. Glen Ellyn, IL: Child Management, Inc., 2000.

**Daredevils and Daydreamers: New Perspectives on Attention-Deficit/Hyperactivity Disorder,** by Barbara Ingersoll, Ph.D. New York: Doubleday, 1998.

**How to Reach and Teach ADD/ADHD Children,** by Sandra F. Rief. West Nyack, NY: Center for Applied Research in Education, 1993.

**Raise Your Child's Social IQ: Stepping Stones to People Skills for Kids,** by Cathi Cohen, LCSW. Silver Spring, MD: Advantage Books, 2000.

**Rewards for Kids! Ready-to-Use Charts & Activities for Positive Parenting,** by Virginia Shiller, Ph.D. Washington, DC: APA LifeTools, 2003.

**Straight Talk About Psychiatric Medications for Kids,** by Timothy Wilens, M.D. New York: Guilford Press, 1999.

**Understanding Girls with ADHD,** by Kathleen Nadeau, Ph.D., Ellen Littman, Ph.D., & Patricia Quinn, M.D. Silver Spring, MD: Advantage Books, 1999.

# SUGGESTED READING FOR KIDS

**The Adventures of Phoebe Flower** (4 volumes), series by Barbara Roberts. Silver Spring, MD: Advantage Books, 1998–2002.

**All Kinds of Minds,** by Mel Levine, M.D. Cambridge, MA: Educators Publishing Service, 1993.

**The Best of "Brakes": An Activity Book for Kids with ADD,** edited by Patricia Quinn, M.D., and Judith Stern. Washington, DC: Magination Press, 2000.

**The Don't-Give-Up Kid (2nd ed.),** by Jeanne Gehret, M.A. Fairport, NY: Verbal Images Press, 1996.

**Help Is on the Way: A Child's Book About ADD,** by Marc Nemiroff, Ph.D., and Jane Annunziata, Psy.D. Washington, DC: Magination Press, 1998.

**Otto Learns About His Medicine: A Story About Medication for Children with ADHD (3rd ed.),** by Matthew Galvin, M.D. Washington, DC: Magination Press, 2001.

**Putting on the Brakes (rev. ed.),** by Patricia Quinn, M.D., and Judith Stern. Washington, DC: Magination Press, 2001.

**The "Putting on the Brakes" Activity Book for Young People with ADHD,** by Patricia Quinn, M.D., and Judith Stern. Washington, DC: Magination Press, 1993.

**Seven Secrets of Highly Successful Kids,** by Peter Kuitenbrouwer. Montreal: Lobster Press, 2001.

**Sparky's Excellent Misadventures: My ADD Journal, By Me (Sparky),** by Phyllis Carpenter and Marti Ford. Washington, DC: Magination Press, 2000.

## ACKNOWLEDGMENT

We would like to express our appreciation to Patricia Quinn, M.D., Melvin D. Levine, M.D., and the many children and parents who have shared their experiences with us and helped us develop the ideas for this book. —K.G.N. and E.B.D.

## ABOUT THE AUTHORS

DR. KATHLEEN NADEAU is a clinical psychologist who has specialized in working with kids and adults with ADHD for many years. She is the director of Chesapeake Psychological Services of Maryland in Silver Spring, MD, and the author of many books on ADHD for kids, teens, adults, and professionals. Dr. Nadeau is a frequent lecturer on topics related to ADHD, both in the US and abroad. Many of the ideas in this book come from her experiences raising her own child with ADHD.

DR. ELLEN DIXON is a licensed clinical psychologist who has long specialized in the differential diagnosis and treatment of attention disorders and related neuropsychological conditions. As a clinician, it has given her great pleasure to work with these children, whom she describes as "lively, appealing, creative, and sometimes blazingly energetic," and their families. Dr. Dixon practices in the Great Bridge area of Chesapeake, Virginia.

## ABOUT THE ILLUSTRATOR

CHARLES BEYL creates humorous illustrations for books, magazines, and newspapers from his studio high atop an old Pennsylvania farmhouse, surrounded by his family, a cuddly black Labrador, two cats, and two prodigious chickens named Helga and Irene.